SELECTED
WRITINGS OF
BAHÁ'U'LLÁH

SELECTED
WRITINGS OF
BAHÁ'U'LLÁH

Bahá'í
PUBLISHING

Wilmette, Illinois

Bahá'í Publishing, Wilmette, IL 60091-2844

First Edition 1942
Second Edition 1975
First Cloth Edition 1979
First Bahá'í Publishing Edition 2005

Library of Congress Cataloging-in-Publication Data
Bahá'u'lláh, 1817–1892
    [Selections. English. 2005]
    Selected writings of Bahá'u'lláh.— 1st Bahá'í Pub. ed.
        p. cm.
    Includes bibliographical references and index.
    ISBN 1-931847-24-X (alk. paper)
    1. Bahai Faith. I. Title.

BP360.A3 2005
297.9'3822—dc22

2005050728

Printed in the United States of America on acid-free paper ∞

Cover design by Robert A. Reddy
Book design by Patrick Falso

Contents

Foreword

"O My servants! My holy, My divinely ordained Revelation may be likened unto an ocean in whose depths are concealed innumerable pearls of great price, of surpassing luster. . . . This most great, this fathomless and surging Ocean is near, astonishingly near, unto you. Behold it is closer to you than your life-vein! Swift as the twinkling of an eye ye can, if ye but wish it, reach and partake of this imperishable favor, this God-given grace, this incorruptible gift, this most potent and unspeakably glorious bounty." So wrote Bahá'u'lláh, whose writings are considered sacred scripture by members of the Bahá'í Faith, an independent world religion that began in Persia during the mid-nineteenth century. Since that time the religion has grown dramatically, and today some five million people representing over two thousand different tribal, ethnic, and racial groups from virtually every country around the globe call themselves Bahá'ís, or followers of Bahá'u'lláh.

Bahá'u'lláh (1817–1892) is the Prophet and Founder of the Bahá'í Faith. His given name was Mírzá Ḥusayn-'Alí, though he was known to most as Bahá'u'lláh, meaning in Arabic "the Glory of God." In reaction to his teachings, which the Muslim clergy of Persia saw as dangerous heresy, Bahá'u'lláh was exiled to various places within the Ottoman Empire, taking him farther and farther from his homeland. Each successive exile was intended to extinguish the flame of his religion yet only served to spread it further. In 1868 he was sent as a prisoner to the fortress city of Acre in the Holy Land and remained in that vicinity until he passed away in 1892. In his will he appointed his eldest son, 'Abdu'l-Bahá (1844–1921), to succeed him as head of the Bahá'í Faith and to interpret the Bahá'í writings. 'Abdu'l-Bahá in turn appointed his eldest grandson, Shoghi Effendi (1897–1957), to be his successor and serve as Guardian of the Cause of God and authorized interpreter of the Bahá'í writings. Today the affairs of the Bahá'í world community are administered by the Universal House of Justice, the supreme governing and legislative body of the religion.

The central teachings of the Bahá'í Faith are the

oneness of God, the oneness of religion, and the oneness of humanity. "The peoples of the world," Bahá'u'lláh wrote, "of whatever race or religion, derive their inspiration from one heavenly Source, and are the subjects of one God."* He proclaimed that religious truth is not absolute but relative, that divine revelation is a continual and progressive process, that all the great religions of the world are divine in origin, and that their missions represent successive stages in the spiritual evolution of society. Bahá'u'lláh taught that the purpose of religion is the promotion of concord and orderly progress in society, and Bahá'í scripture delineates the basic outline of institutions necessary for establishing peace and world order.

Bahá'í scripture also provides specific guidance that identifies the basic purpose of human life, which is to know and to worship God and to carry forward an "ever-advancing civilization" by striving to bring about the oneness of humanity, world peace, and world order. For example, Bahá'í scripture calls for fostering good character and developing spiritual qualities such as honesty, trustworthiness, compassion, and justice, to name but a few. These virtues are latent in every

---

* *Gleanings from the Writings of Bahá'u'lláh,* p. 217.

soul but must be developed through prayer, meditation, and work done in a spirit of service to humanity—all of which are, for Bahá'ís, expressions of the worship of God. Bahá'u'lláh calls for eradicating all prejudices, including those of race, creed, class, nationality, and sex so that the oneness of humanity may be realized. He also calls for the systematic elimination of all superstition and exhorts us to balance the material and spiritual aspects of life, which rest on an understanding of the truth and of the harmony of science and religion as two facets of the truth. He encourages the development of every individual's unique capacities and talents through the pursuit of knowledge and the acquisition of skills. The practice of a trade or profession is required not only for personal satisfaction but also for the enrichment of society as a whole. He calls for the full participation of both women and men in all aspects of community life, including elective and administrative processes and decision-making, in implementing the principle of equal opportunities, rights, and privileges for both sexes. Additionally, he calls for fostering the principle of universal compulsory education and for the elimination of extremes of wealth and poverty.

The selections in this volume are indeed but a drop from the fathomless ocean of the writings of

Bahá'u'lláh. They provide a brief overview of his teachings about the fulfillment of other religions, God and his Messengers, the path to God, spiritual aspects of the world order of Bahá'u'lláh, the soul and life after death, and the renewal of God's covenant with humanity. It is hoped that the reader will be moved to explore the vast ocean of Bahá'u'lláh's words more fully by going to the works from which these passages were selected.

The Day of God

1

he purpose underlying all creation is the revelation of this most sublime, this most holy Day, the Day known as the Day of God, in His Books and Scriptures—the Day which all the Prophets, and the Chosen Ones, and the holy ones, have wished to witness.

2

his Day a door is open wider than both heaven and earth. The eye of the mercy of Him Who is the Desire of the worlds is turned towards all men. An act, however infinitesimal, is, when viewed in the mirror of the knowledge of God, mightier than a mountain. Every drop proffered in His path is as the sea in that mirror. For this is the Day which the one true God, glorified be He, hath announced in all His Books unto His Prophets and His Messengers.

3

his is the Chief of all days and the King thereof. Great is the blessedness of him who hath attained, through the sweet savor of these days, unto everlasting life, and who, with the most great steadfastness, hath arisen to aid the Cause of Him Who is the King of Names. Such a man is as the eye to the body of mankind.

4

eerless is this Day, for it is as the eye to past ages and centuries, and as a light unto the darkness of the times.

5

od the true One is My Witness! This is the Day whereon it is incumbent upon everyone that seeth to behold, and every ear that hearkeneth to hear, and every heart that understandeth to perceive, and every tongue that speaketh to proclaim unto all who are in heaven and on earth, this holy, this exalted, and all-highest Name.

6

he potentialities inherent in the station of man, the full measure of his destiny on earth, the innate excellence of his reality, must all be manifested in this promised Day of God.

God and His Manifestations

7

 auded be Thy name, O Lord my God! How great is Thy might and Thy sovereignty; how vast Thy strength and Thy dominion!

8

ll praise, O my God, be to Thee Who art the Source of all glory and majesty, of greatness and honor, of sovereignty and dominion, of loftiness and grace, of awe and power.

9

od testifieth to the unity of His Godhood and to the singleness of His own Being. On the throne of eternity, from the inaccessible heights of His station, His tongue proclaimeth that there is none other God but Him. He Himself, independently of all else, hath ever been a witness unto His own oneness, the revealer of His own nature, the glorifier of His own essence. He, verily, is the All-Powerful, the Almighty, the Beauteous.

He is supreme over His servants, and standeth over His creatures. In His hand is the source of authority and truth. He maketh men alive by His signs, and causeth them to die through His wrath. He shall not be asked of His doings and His might is equal unto all things. He is the Potent, the All-Subduing.

He holdeth within His grasp the empire of all things, and on His right hand is fixed the Kingdom of His Revelation. His power, verily, embraceth the whole of creation. Victory and overlordship are His; all might and dominion are His; all glory and greatness are His. He, of a truth, is the All-Glorious, the Most Powerful, the Unconditioned.

10

xalted, immeasurably exalted, art Thou above the strivings of mortal man to unravel Thy mystery, to describe Thy glory, or even to hint at the nature of Thine Essence. For whatever such strivings may accomplish, they never can hope to transcend the limitations imposed upon Thy creatures, inasmuch as these efforts are actuated by Thy decree, and are begotten of Thine invention. The loftiest sentiments which the holiest of saints can express in praise of Thee, and the deepest wisdom which the most learned of men can utter in their attempts to comprehend Thy nature, all revolve around that Center Which is wholly subjected to Thy sovereignty, Which adoreth Thy Beauty, and is propelled through the movement of Thy Pen.

11

xalted, immeasurably exalted art Thou above any attempt to measure the greatness of Thy Cause, above any comparison that one may seek to make, above the efforts of the human tongue to utter its import! From everlasting Thou hast existed, alone with no one else beside Thee, and wilt, to everlasting, continue to remain the same, in the sublimity of Thine essence and the inaccessible heights of Thy glory.
And when Thou didst purpose to make Thyself known unto men, Thou didst successively reveal the Manifestations of Thy Cause, and ordained each to be a sign of Thy Revelation among Thy people, and the Dayspring of Thine invisible Self amidst Thy creatures. . . .

12

 now thou of a certainty that the Unseen can in no wise incarnate His Essence and reveal it unto men. He is, and hath ever been, immensely exalted beyond all that can either be recounted or perceived. From His retreat of glory His voice is ever proclaiming: "Verily, I am God; there is none other God besides Me, the All-Knowing, the All-Wise. I have manifested Myself unto men, and have sent down Him Who is the Dayspring of the signs of My Revelation. Through Him I have caused all creation to testify that there is none other God except Him, the Incomparable, the All-Informed, the All-Wise." He Who is everlastingly hidden from the eyes of men can never be known except through His Manifestation, and His Manifestation can adduce no greater proof of the truth of His Mission than the proof of His own Person.

13

he door of the knowledge of the Ancient of Days being thus closed in the face of all beings, the Source of infinite grace, according to His saying, "His grace hath transcended all things; My grace hath encompassed them all," hath caused those luminous Gems of Holiness to appear out of the realm of the spirit, in the noble form of the human temple, and be made manifest unto all men, that they may impart unto the world the mysteries of the unchangeable Being, and tell of the subtleties of His imperishable Essence.

These sanctified Mirrors, these Daysprings of ancient glory, are, one and all, the Exponents on earth of Him Who is the central Orb of the universe, its Essence and ultimate Purpose. From Him proceed their knowledge and power; from Him is derived their sovereignty. The beauty of their countenance is but a reflection of His image, and their revelation a sign of His deathless glory. They are the Treasuries of Divine knowledge, and the Repositories of celestial wisdom. Through them is transmitted a grace that is infinite, and by them is revealed the Light that can never fade. . . .

14

now thou assuredly that the essence of all the Prophets of God is one and the same. Their unity is absolute. God, the Creator, saith: There is no distinction whatsoever among the Bearers of My Message. They all have but one purpose; their secret is the same secret. To prefer one in honor to another, to exalt certain ones above the rest, is in no wise to be permitted. Every true Prophet hath regarded His Message as fundamentally the same as the Revelation of every other Prophet gone before Him. If any man, therefore, should fail to comprehend this truth, and should consequently indulge in vain and unseemly language, no one whose sight is keen and whose understanding is enlightened would ever allow such idle talk to cause him to waver in his belief.

15

eware, O believers in the Unity of God, lest ye be tempted to make any distinction between any of the Manifestations of His Cause, or to discriminate against the signs that have accompanied and proclaimed their Revelation. This indeed is the true meaning of Divine Unity, if ye be of them that apprehend and believe this truth. Be ye assured, moreover, that the works and acts of each and every one of these Manifestations of God, nay whatever pertaineth unto them, and whatsoever they may manifest in the future, are all ordained by God, and are a reflection of His Will and Purpose. Whoso maketh the slightest possible difference between their persons, their words, their messages, their acts and manners, hath indeed disbelieved in God, hath repudiated His signs, and betrayed the Cause of His Messengers.

16

rom the foregoing passages and allusions it hath been made indubitably clear that in the kingdoms of earth and heaven there must needs be manifested a Being, an Essence Who shall act as a Manifestation and Vehicle for the transmission of the grace of the Divinity Itself, the Sovereign Lord of all. Through the Teachings of this Daystar of Truth every man will advance and develop until he attaineth the station at which he can manifest all the potential forces with which his inmost true self hath been endowed. It is for this very purpose that in every age and dispensation the Prophets of God and His chosen Ones have appeared amongst men, and have evinced such power as is born of God and such might as only the Eternal can reveal.

The Path to God

17

he beginning of all things is the knowledge of God, and the end of all things is strict observance of whatsoever hath been sent down from the empyrean of the Divine Will that pervadeth all that is in the heavens and all that is on the earth.

18

o man shall attain the shores of the ocean of true understanding except he be detached from all that is in heaven and on earth. . . .

The essence of these words is this: they that tread the path of faith, they that thirst for the wine of certitude, must cleanse themselves of all that is earthly—their ears from idle talk, their minds from vain imaginings, their hearts from worldly affections, their eyes from that which perisheth. They should put their trust in God, and, holding fast unto Him, follow in His way. Then will they be made worthy of the effulgent glories of the sun of divine knowledge and understanding, and become the recipients of a grace that is infinite and unseen, inasmuch as man can never hope to attain unto the knowledge of the All-Glorious, can never quaff from the stream of divine knowledge and wisdom, can never enter the abode of immortality, nor partake of the cup of divine nearness and favor, unless and until he ceases to regard the words and deeds of mortal men as a standard for the true understanding and recognition of God and His Prophets.

19

now verily that Knowledge is of two kinds: Divine and Satanic. The one welleth out from the fountain of divine inspiration; the other is but a reflection of vain and obscure thoughts. The source of the former is God Himself; the motive-force of the latter the whisperings of selfish desire. The one is guided by the principle: "Fear ye God, God will teach you"; the other is but a confirmation of the truth: "Knowledge is the most grievous veil between man and his Creator." The former bringeth forth the fruit of patience, of longing desire, of true understanding, and love; whilst the latter can yield naught but arrogance, vainglory and conceit.

20

 now assuredly that just as thou firmly believest that the Word of God, exalted be His glory, endureth for ever, thou must, likewise, believe with undoubting faith that its meaning can never be exhausted. They who are its appointed interpreters, they whose hearts are the repositories of its secrets, are, however, the only ones who can comprehend its manifold wisdom. Whoso, while reading the Sacred Scriptures, is tempted to choose therefrom whatever may suit him with which to challenge the authority of the Representative of God among men, is, indeed, as one dead, though to outward seeming he may walk and converse with his neighbors, and share with them their food and their drink.

Oh, would that the world could believe Me! Were

all the things that lie enshrined within the heart of Bahá,* and which the Lord, His God, the Lord of all names, hath taught Him, to be unveiled to mankind, every man on earth would be dumbfounded.

How great the multitude of truths which the garment of words can never contain! How vast the number of such verities as no expression can adequately describe, whose significance can never be unfolded, and to which not even the remotest allusions can be made! How manifold are the truths which must remain unuttered until the appointed time is come! Even as it hath been said: "Not everything that a man knoweth can be disclosed, nor can everything that he can disclose be regarded as timely, nor can every timely utterance be considered as suited to the capacity of those who hear it."

Of these truths some can be disclosed only to the extent of the capacity of the repositories of the light of Our knowledge, and the recipients of Our hidden grace. We beseech God to strengthen thee with His power, and enable thee to recognize Him Who is the Source of all knowledge, that thou mayest detach thyself from all human learning, for, "what would it profit any man to strive after learning when he hath

---

* Literally, glory, splendor, light; an allusion to Bahá'u'lláh.

already found and recognized Him Who is the Object of all knowledge?" Cleave to the Root of Knowledge, and to Him Who is the Fountain thereof, that thou mayest find thyself independent of all who claim to be well versed in human learning, and whose claim no clear proof, nor the testimony of any enlightening book, can support.

21

now thou that he is truly learned who hath acknowledged My Revelation, and drunk from the Ocean of My knowledge, and soared in the atmosphere of My love, and cast away all else besides Me, and taken firm hold on that which hath been sent down from the Kingdom of My wondrous utterance. He, verily, is even as an eye unto mankind, and as the spirit of life unto the body of all creation. Glorified be the All-Merciful Who hath enlightened him, and caused him to arise and serve His great and mighty Cause. Verily, such a man is blessed by the Concourse on high, and by them who dwell within the Tabernacle of Grandeur, who have quaffed My sealed Wine in My Name, the Omnipotent, the All-Powerful.

22

or every one of you his paramount duty is to choose for himself that on which no other may infringe and none usurp from him. Such a thing—and to this the Almighty is My witness—is the love of God, could ye but perceive it.

23

o man that seeketh Us will We ever disappoint, neither shall he that hath set his face towards Us be denied access unto Our court. . . .

24

f it be your wish, O people, to know God and to discover the greatness of His might, look, then, upon Me with Mine own eyes, and not with the eyes of any one besides Me.

25

My servant, who hast sought the good-pleasure of God and clung to His love on the Day when all except a few who were endued with insight have broken away from Him! May God, through His grace, recompense thee with a generous, an incorruptible and everlasting reward, inasmuch as thou hast sought Him on the Day when eyes were blinded.

26

 wayfarer in the path of God! Take thou thy portion of the ocean of His grace, and deprive not thyself of the things that lie hidden in its depths. Be thou of them that have partaken of its treasures. A dewdrop out of this ocean would, if shed upon all that are in the heavens and on the earth, suffice to enrich them with the bounty of God, the Almighty, the All-Knowing, the All-Wise. With the hands of renunciation draw forth from its life-giving waters, and sprinkle therewith all created things, that they may be cleansed from all man-made limitations and may approach the mighty seat of God, this hallowed and resplendent Spot.

27

 hat the heart is the throne, in which the Revelation of God the All-Merciful is centered, is attested by the holy utterances which We have formerly revealed.

Among them is this saying: "Earth and heaven cannot contain Me; what can alone contain Me is the heart of him that believeth in Me, and is faithful to My Cause." How often hath the human heart, which is the recipient of the light of God and the seat of the revelation of the All-Merciful, erred from Him Who is the Source of that light and the Wellspring of that revelation. It is the waywardness of the heart that removeth it far from God, and condemneth it to remoteness from Him. Those hearts, however, that are aware of His Presence, are close to Him, and are to be regarded as having drawn nigh unto His throne.

Consider, moreover, how frequently doth man become forgetful of his own self, whilst God remaineth, through His all-encompassing knowledge, aware of His creature, and continueth to shed upon him the manifest radiance of His glory. It is evident, therefore, that, in such circumstances, He is closer to him than his own self. He will, indeed, so remain for ever, for, whereas the one true God knoweth all things, perceiveth all things, and comprehendeth all things, mortal man is prone to err, and is ignorant of the mysteries that lie enfolded within him. . . .

28

lessed are they that have soared on the wings of detachment and attained the station which, as ordained by God, overshadoweth the entire creation, whom neither the vain imaginations of the learned, nor the multitude of the hosts of the earth have succeeded in deflecting from His Cause. Who is there among you, O people, who will renounce the world, and draw nigh unto God, the Lord of all names? Where is he to be found who, through the power of My name that transcendeth all created things, will cast away the things that men possess, and cling, with all his might, to the things which God, the Knower of the unseen and of the seen, hath bidden him observe? Thus hath His bounty been sent down unto men, His testimony fulfilled, and His proof shone forth above the Horizon of mercy. Rich is the prize that shall be won by him who hath believed and exclaimed: "Lauded art Thou, O Beloved of all worlds! Magnified be Thy name, O Thou the Desire of every understanding heart!"

29

ear asunder, in My Name, the veils that have grievously blinded your vision, and, through the power born of your belief in the unity of God, scatter the idols of vain imitation. Enter, then, the holy paradise of the good-pleasure of the All-Merciful. Sanctify your souls from whatsoever is not of God, and taste ye the sweetness of rest within the pale of His vast and mighty Revelation, and beneath the shadow of His supreme and infallible authority. Suffer not yourselves to be wrapt in the dense veils of your selfish desires, inasmuch as I have perfected in every one of you My creation, so that the excellence of My handiwork may be fully revealed unto men. It follows, therefore, that every man hath been, and will continue to be, able of himself to appreciate the Beauty of God, the Glorified. Had he not been endowed with such a capacity, how could he be called to account for his failure? If, in the Day when all the peoples of the earth will be gathered together, any man should, whilst standing in the presence of God, be asked: "Wherefore hast thou disbelieved in My Beauty and turned away from My Self," and if such a man should reply and say: "Inasmuch as all men have erred, and none hath been found willing to turn his face to the Truth, I, too, following their example, have grievously failed to recognize the Beauty of the Eternal," such a plea will, assuredly, be rejected. For the faith of no man can be conditioned by any one except himself.

30

 now thou that all men have been created in the nature made by God, the Guardian, the Self-Subsisting. Unto each one hath been prescribed a pre-ordained measure, as decreed in God's mighty and guarded Tablets. All that which ye potentially possess can, however, be manifested only as a result of your own volition. Your own acts testify to this truth.

31

 ay: O people! The Lamp of God is burning; take heed, lest the fierce winds of your disobedience extinguish its light. Now is the time to arise and magnify the Lord, your God. Strive not after bodily comforts, and keep your heart pure and stainless. The Evil One is lying in wait, ready to entrap you. Gird yourselves against his wicked devices, and, led by the light of the name of the one true God, deliver yourselves from the darkness that surroundeth you. Center your thoughts in the Well-Beloved, rather than in your own selves.

32

lessed is the man that hath acknowledged his belief in God and in His signs, and recognized that "He shall not be asked of His doings." Such a recognition hath been made by God the ornament of every belief, and its very foundation. Upon it must depend the acceptance of every goodly deed. Fasten your eyes upon it, that haply the whisperings of the rebellious may not cause you to slip.

Were He to decree as lawful the thing which from time immemorial had been forbidden, and forbid that which had, at all times, been regarded as lawful, to none is given the right to question His authority. Whoso will hesitate, though it be for less than a moment, should be regarded as a transgressor.

Whoso hath not recognized this sublime and

fundamental verity, and hath failed to attain this most exalted station, the winds of doubt will agitate him, and the sayings of the infidels will distract his soul. He that hath acknowledged this principle will be endowed with the most perfect constancy. All honor to this all-glorious station, the remembrance of which adorneth every exalted Tablet. Such is the teaching which God bestoweth on you, a teaching that will deliver you from all manner of doubt and perplexity, and enable you to attain unto salvation both in this world and in the next. He, verily, is the Ever-Forgiving, the Most Bountiful.

33

he ordinances of God have been sent down from the heaven of His most august Revelation. All must diligently observe them. Man's supreme distinction, his real advancement, his final victory, have always depended, and will continue to depend, upon them. Whoso keepeth the commandments of God shall attain everlasting felicity.

A twofold obligation resteth upon him who hath recognized the Dayspring of the Unity of God, and acknowledged the truth of Him Who is the Manifestation of His oneness. The first is steadfastness in His love, such steadfastness that neither the clamor of the enemy nor the claims of the idle pretender can deter him from cleaving unto Him Who is the Eternal Truth, a steadfastness that taketh no account of them whatever. The second is strict observance of the laws He hath prescribed—laws which He hath always ordained, and will continue to ordain, unto men, and through which the truth may be distinguished and separated from falsehood.

34

henever My laws appear like the sun in the heaven of Mine utterance, they must be faithfully obeyed by all, though My decree be such as to cause the heaven of every religion to be cleft asunder. He doth what He pleaseth. He chooseth; and none may question His choice. Whatsoever He, the Well-Beloved, ordaineth, the same is, verily, beloved. To this He Who is the Lord of all creation beareth Me witness. Whoso hath inhaled the sweet fragrance of the All-Merciful, and recognized the Source of this utterance, will welcome with his own eyes the shafts of the enemy, that he may establish the truth of the laws of God amongst men. Well is it with him that hath turned thereunto, and apprehended the meaning of His decisive decree.

35

isencumber yourselves of all attachment to this world and the vanities thereof. Beware that ye approach them not, inasmuch as they prompt you to walk after your own lusts and covetous desires, and hinder you from entering the straight and glorious Path.

Know ye that by "the world" is meant your unawareness of Him Who is your Maker, and your absorption in aught else but Him. The "life to come," on the other hand, signifieth the things that give you a safe approach to God, the All-Glorious, the Incomparable. Whatsoever deterreth you, in this Day, from loving God is nothing but the world. Flee it, that ye may be numbered with the blest. Should a man wish to adorn himself with the ornaments of the earth, to wear its apparels, or partake of the benefits it can bestow, no harm can befall him, if he alloweth nothing whatever to intervene between him and God, for God hath ordained every good thing, whether created in the heavens or in the earth, for such of His servants as truly believe in Him. Eat ye, O people, of the good things which God hath allowed you, and deprive not yourselves from His wondrous bounties. Render thanks and praise unto Him, and be of them that are truly thankful.

36

ut, O my brother, when a true seeker determineth to take the step of search in the path leading to the knowledge of the Ancient of Days, he must, before all else, cleanse and purify his heart, which is the seat of the revelation of the inner mysteries of God, from the obscuring dust of all acquired knowledge, and the allusions of the embodiments of satanic fancy. He must purge his breast, which is the sanctuary of the abiding love of the Beloved, of every defilement, and sanctify his soul from all that pertaineth to water and clay, from all shadowy and ephemeral attachments. He must so cleanse his heart that no remnant of either love or hate may linger therein, lest that love blindly incline him to error, or that hate repel him away from the truth. Even as thou dost witness in this day how most of the people, because of such love and hate, are bereft of the immortal Face, have strayed far from the Embodiments of the divine mysteries, and, shepherdless, are roaming through the wilderness of oblivion and error. That seeker must at all times put his trust in God, must renounce the peoples of the earth, detach himself from the world of dust, and cleave unto Him Who is the Lord of Lords. He must never seek to exalt himself above any one, must wash away from the tablet of his heart every trace of pride and vainglory, must cling unto patience and resignation, observe silence, and refrain from idle talk. For the tongue is a smoldering fire, and excess of speech a deadly poison. Material fire consumeth the body, whereas the fire of the tongue devoureth both heart and soul. The force of the former lasteth but for a time, whilst the effects of the latter endure a century.

That seeker should also regard backbiting as grievous error, and keep himself aloof from its dominion, inasmuch as backbiting quencheth the light of the heart, and extinguisheth the life of the soul. He should be content with little, and be freed from all inordinate desire. He should treasure the companionship of those that have renounced the world, and regard avoidance of boastful and worldly people a precious benefit. At the dawn of every day he should commune with God, and with all his soul persevere in the quest of his Beloved. He should consume every wayward thought with the flame of His loving mention, and, with the swiftness of lightning, pass by all else save Him. He should succor the dispossessed, and never withhold his favor from the destitute. He should show kindness to animals, how much more unto his fellow-man, to him who is endowed with the power of utterance. He should not hesitate to offer up his life for his Beloved, nor allow the censure of the people to turn him away from the Truth. He should not wish for others that which he doth not wish for himself, nor promise that which he doth not fulfill. With all his heart should the seeker avoid fellowship with evil doers, and pray for the remission of their sins. He should forgive the sinful, and never despise his low estate, for none knoweth what his own end shall be. How often hath a sinner, at the hour of death, attained to the essence of faith, and, quaffing the immortal draught, hath taken his flight unto the celestial Concourse. And how often hath a devout believer, at the hour of his soul's ascension, been so changed as to fall into the nethermost fire. Our purpose in revealing these convincing and weighty utterances is to impress upon the seeker that he should regard all else beside God as transient, and count all things save Him, Who is the Object of all adoration, as utter nothingness.

37

e generous in prosperity, and thankful in adversity. Be worthy of the trust of thy neighbor, and look upon him with a bright and friendly face. Be a treasure to the poor, an admonisher to the rich, an answerer to the cry of the needy, a preserver of the sanctity of thy pledge. Be fair in thy judgment, and guarded in thy speech. Be unjust to no man, and show all meekness to all men. Be as a lamp unto them that walk in darkness, a joy to the sorrowful, a sea for the thirsty, a haven for the distressed, an upholder and defender of the victim of oppression. Let integrity and uprightness distinguish all thine acts. Be a home for the stranger, a balm to the suffering, a tower of strength for the fugitive. Be eyes to the blind, and a guiding light unto the feet of the erring. Be an ornament to the countenance of truth, a crown to the brow of fidelity, a pillar of the temple of righteousness, a breath of life to the body of mankind, an ensign of the hosts of justice, a luminary above the horizon of virtue, a dew to the soil of the human heart, an ark on the ocean of knowledge, a sun in the heaven of bounty, a gem on the diadem of wisdom, a shining light in the firmament of thy generation, a fruit upon the tree of humility.

38

eautify your tongues, O people, with truthfulness, and adorn your souls with the ornament of honesty. Beware, O people, that ye deal not treacherously with any one. Be ye the trustees of God amongst His creatures, and the emblems of His generosity amidst His people. They that follow their lusts and corrupt inclinations, have erred and dissipated their efforts. They, indeed, are of the lost. Strive, O people, that your eyes may be directed towards the mercy of God, that your hearts may be attuned to His wondrous remembrance, that your souls may rest confidently upon His grace and bounty, that your feet may tread the path of His good-pleasure. Such are the counsels which I bequeath unto you. Would that ye might follow My counsels!

39

he true seeker hunteth naught but the object of his quest, and the lover hath no desire save union with his beloved. Nor shall the seeker reach his goal unless he sacrifice all things. That is, whatever he hath seen, and heard, and understood, all must he set at naught, that he may enter the realm of the spirit, which is the City of God. Labor is needed, if we are to seek Him; ardor is needed, if we are to drink of the honey of reunion with Him; and if we taste of this cup, we shall cast away the world.

On this journey the traveler abideth in every land and dwelleth in every region. In every face, he seeketh the beauty of the Friend; in every country he looketh for the Beloved. He joineth every company, and seeketh fellowship with every soul, that haply in some mind he may uncover the secret of the Friend, or in some face he may behold the beauty of the Loved One.

40

ay: Let truthfulness and courtesy be your adorning. Suffer not yourselves to be deprived of the robe of forbearance and justice, that the sweet savors of holiness may be wafted from your hearts upon all created things. Say: Beware, O people of Bahá,* lest ye walk in the ways of them whose words differ from their deeds. Strive that ye may be enabled to manifest to the peoples of the earth the signs of God, and to mirror forth His commandments. Let your acts be a guide unto all mankind, for the professions of most men, be they high or low, differ from their conduct. It is through your deeds that ye can distinguish yourselves

---

* Literally, glory, splendor, light; an allusion to Bahá'u'lláh.

from others. Through them the brightness of your light can be shed upon the whole earth. Happy is the man that heedeth My counsel, and keepeth the precepts prescribed by Him Who is the All-Knowing, the All-Wise.

41

ling ye to the hem of virtue, and hold fast to the cord of trustworthiness and piety. Concern yourselves with the things that benefit mankind, and not with your corrupt and selfish desires. O ye followers of this Wronged One! Ye are the shepherds of mankind; liberate ye your flocks from the wolves of evil passions and desires, and adorn them with the ornament of the fear of God. This is the firm commandment which hath, at this moment, flowed out from the Pen of Him Who is the Ancient of Days. By the righteousness of God! The sword of a virtuous character and upright conduct is sharper than blades of steel.

42

o thou beseech God to enable thee to remain steadfast in this path, and to aid thee to guide the peoples of the world to Him Who is the manifest and sovereign Ruler, Who hath revealed Himself in a distinct attire, Who giveth utterance to a Divine and specific Message. This is the essence of faith and certitude. They that are the worshipers of the idol which their imaginations have carved, and who call it Inner Reality, such men are in truth accounted among the heathen. To this hath the All-Merciful borne witness in His Tablets. He, verily, is the All-Knowing, the All-Wise.

43

 My servants! Sorrow not if, in these days and on this earthly plane, things contrary to your wishes have been ordained and manifested by God, for days of blissful joy, of heavenly delight, are assuredly in store for you. Worlds, holy and spiritually glorious, will be unveiled to your eyes. You are destined by Him, in this world and hereafter, to partake of their benefits, to share in their joys, and to obtain a portion of their sustaining grace. To each and every one of them you will, no doubt, attain.

44

 hen the victory arriveth, every man shall profess himself as believer and shall hasten to the shelter of God's Faith. Happy are they who in the days of world-encompassing trials have stood fast in the Cause and refused to swerve from its truth.

45

evile ye not one another. We, verily, have come to unite and weld together all that dwell on earth. Unto this beareth witness what the ocean of Mine utterance hath revealed amongst men, and yet most of the people have gone astray. If anyone revile you, or trouble touch you, in the path of God, be patient, and put your trust in Him Who heareth, Who seeth. He, in truth, witnesseth, and perceiveth, and doeth what He pleaseth, through the power of His sovereignty. He, verily, is the Lord of strength, and of might. In the Book of God, the Mighty, the Great, ye have been forbidden to engage in contention and conflict. Lay fast hold on whatever will profit you, and profit the peoples of the world. Thus commandeth you the King of Eternity, Who is manifest in His Most Great Name. He, verily, is the Ordainer, the All-Wise.

Unity, Peace, and Justice

46

he All-Knowing Physician hath His finger on the pulse of mankind. He perceiveth the disease, and prescribeth, in His unerring wisdom, the remedy. Every age hath its own problem, and every soul its particular aspiration. The remedy the world needeth in its present-day afflictions can never be the same as that which a subsequent age may require. Be anxiously concerned with the needs of the age ye live in, and center your deliberations on its exigencies and requirements.

47

hat which God hath ordained as the sovereign remedy and mightiest instrument for the healing of the world is the union of all its peoples in one universal Cause, one common Faith. This can in no wise be achieved except through the power of a skilled, an all-powerful, and inspired Physician. By My life! This is the truth, and all else naught but error.

48

he Prophets of God should be regarded as physicians whose task is to foster the well-being of the world and its peoples, that, through the spirit of oneness, they may heal the sickness of a divided humanity. To none is given the right to question their words or disparage their conduct, for they are the only ones who can claim to have understood the patient and to have correctly diagnosed its ailments. No man, however acute his perception, can ever hope to reach the heights which the wisdom and understanding of the Divine Physician have attained. Little wonder, then, if the treatment prescribed by the physician in this day should not be found to be identical with that which he prescribed before. How could it be otherwise when the ills affecting the sufferer necessitate at every stage of his sickness a special remedy? In like manner, every time the Prophets of God have illumined the world with the resplendent radiance of the Daystar of Divine knowledge, they have invariably summoned its peoples to embrace the light of God through such means as best befitted the exigencies of the age in which they appeared. They were thus able to scatter the darkness of ignorance, and to shed upon the world the glory of their own knowledge. It is towards the inmost essence of these Prophets, therefore, that the eye of every man of discernment must be directed, inasmuch as their one and only purpose hath always been to guide the erring, and give peace to the afflicted. . . . These are not days of prosperity and triumph. The whole of mankind is in the grip of manifold ills. Strive, therefore, to save its life through the wholesome medicine which the almighty hand of the unerring Physician hath prepared.

49

 he Ancient Beauty hath consented to be bound with chains that mankind may be released from its bondage, and hath accepted to be made a prisoner within this most mighty Stronghold that the whole world may attain unto true liberty. He hath drained to its dregs the cup of sorrow, that all the peoples of the earth may attain unto abiding joy, and be filled with gladness. This is of the mercy of your Lord, the Compassionate, the Most Merciful. We have accepted to be abased, O believers in the Unity of God, that ye may be exalted, and have suffered manifold afflictions, that ye might prosper and flourish. He Who hath come to build anew the whole world, behold, how they that have joined partners with God have forced Him to dwell within the most desolate of cities!

50

he One true God beareth Me witness, and His creatures will testify, that not for a moment did I allow Myself to be hidden from the eyes of men, nor did I consent to shield My person from their injury. Before the face of all men I have arisen, and bidden them fulfill My pleasure. My object is none other than the betterment of the world and the tranquillity of its peoples. The well-being of mankind, its peace and security, are unattainable unless and until its unity is firmly established. This unity can never be achieved so long as the counsels which the Pen of the Most High hath revealed are suffered to pass unheeded.

Through the power of the words He hath uttered the whole of the human race can be illumined with the light of unity, and the remembrance of His Name is able to set on fire the hearts of all men, and burn away the veils that intervene between them and His glory. One righteous act is endowed with a potency that can so elevate the dust as to cause it to pass beyond the heaven of heavens. It can tear every bond asunder, and hath the power to restore the force that hath spent itself and vanished. . . .

Be pure, O people of God, be pure; be righteous, be righteous. . . . Say: O people of God! That which can ensure the victory of Him Who is the Eternal Truth, His hosts and helpers on earth, have been set down in the sacred Books and Scriptures, and are as clear and manifest as the sun. These hosts are such righteous deeds, such conduct and character, as are acceptable in His sight. Whoso ariseth, in this Day, to aid Our Cause, and summoneth to his assistance the hosts of a praiseworthy character and upright conduct, the influence flowing from such an action will, most certainly, be diffused throughout the whole world.

51

 ow vast is the tabernacle of the Cause of God! It hath overshadowed all the peoples and kindreds of the earth, and will, ere-long, gather together the whole of mankind beneath its shelter. Thy day of service is now come. Countless Tablets bear the testimony of the bounties vouchsafed unto thee. Arise for the triumph of My Cause, and, through the power of thine utterance, subdue the hearts of men. Thou must show forth that which will ensure the peace and the well-being of the miserable and the downtrodden. Gird up the loins of thine endeavor, that perchance thou mayest release the captive from his chains, and enable him to attain unto true liberty.

Justice is, in this day, bewailing its plight, and Equity groaneth beneath the yoke of oppression. The thick clouds of tyranny have darkened the face of the earth, and enveloped its peoples. Through the movement of Our Pen of glory We have, at the bidding of the omnipotent Ordainer, breathed a new life into every human frame, and instilled into every word a fresh potency. All created things proclaim the evidences of this world-wide regeneration. This is the most great, the most joyful tidings imparted by the Pen of this Wronged One to mankind. Wherefore fear ye, O My well-beloved ones? Who is it that can dismay you? A touch of moisture sufficeth to dissolve the hardened clay out of which this perverse generation is molded. The mere act of your gathering together is enough to scatter the forces of these vain and worthless people. . . .

Every man of insight will, in this day, readily admit that the counsels which the Pen of this Wronged One hath revealed constitute the supreme animating power for the advancement of the world and the exaltation of its peoples. Arise, O people, and, by the power of God's might, resolve to gain the victory over your own selves, that haply the whole earth may be freed and sanctified from its servitude to the gods of its idle fancies—gods that have inflicted such loss upon, and are responsible for the misery of their wretched worshipers. These idols form the obstacle that impedeth man in his efforts to advance in the path of perfection. We cherish the hope that the Hand of divine power may lend its assistance to mankind and deliver it from its state of grievous abasement.

In one of the Tablets these words have been revealed: O people of God! Do not busy yourselves in your own concerns; let your thoughts be fixed upon that which will rehabilitate the fortunes of mankind and sanctify the hearts and souls of men. This can best be achieved through pure and holy deeds, through a virtuous life and a goodly behavior. Valiant acts will ensure the triumph of this Cause, and a saintly character will reinforce its power. Cleave unto righteousness, O people of Bahá!* This, verily, is the commandment which this Wronged One hath given unto you, and the first choice of His unrestrained Will for every one of you.

---

* Literally, glory, splendor, light; an allusion to Bahá'u'lláh.

52

he purpose of the one true God, exalted be His glory, hath been to bring forth the Mystic Gems out of the mine of man—they Who are the Dawning-Places of His Cause and the Repositories of the pearls of His knowledge; for, God Himself, glorified be He, is the Unseen, the One concealed and hidden from the eyes of men. Consider what the Merciful hath revealed in the Qur'án: No vision taketh in Him, but He taketh in all vision, and He is the Subtile, the All-Informed!"

That the divers communions of the earth, and the manifold systems of religious belief, should never be allowed to foster the feelings of animosity among men, is, in this Day, of the essence of the Faith of God and His Religion. These principles and laws, these firmly established and mighty systems, have proceeded from one Source, and are rays of one Light. That they differ one from another is to be attributed to the varying requirements of the ages in which they were promulgated.

Gird up the loins of your endeavor, O people of Bahá,* that haply the tumult of religious dissension and strife that agitateth the peoples of the earth may be stilled, that every trace of it may be completely obliterated. For the love of God, and them that serve Him, arise to aid this sublime and momentous Revelation. Religious fanaticism and hatred are a world-devouring fire, whose violence none can quench. The Hand of Divine power can, alone, deliver mankind from this desolating affliction. . . .

The utterance of God is a lamp, whose light is these words: Ye are the fruits of one tree, and the leaves of one branch. Deal ye one with another with the utmost love and harmony, with friendliness and fellowship. He Who is the Daystar of Truth beareth Me witness! So powerful is the light of unity that it can illuminate the whole earth. The One true God, He Who knoweth all things, Himself testifieth to the truth of these words.

----

* Literally, glory, splendor, light; an allusion to Bahá'u'lláh.

53

eware lest the desires of the flesh and of a corrupt inclination provoke divisions among you. Be ye as the fingers of one hand, the members of one body. Thus counseleth you the Pen of Revelation, if ye be of them that believe.

54

 friends! Be not careless of the virtues with which ye have been endowed, neither be neglectful of your high destiny. Suffer not your labors to be wasted through the vain imaginations which certain hearts have devised. Ye are the stars of the heaven of understanding, the breeze that stirreth at the break of day, the soft-flowing waters upon which must depend the very life of all men, the letters inscribed upon His sacred scroll. With the utmost unity, and in a spirit of perfect fellowship, exert yourselves, that ye may be enabled to achieve that which beseemeth this Day of God. Verily I say, strife and dissension, and whatsoever the mind of man abhorreth are entirely unworthy of his station. Center your energies in the propagation of the Faith of God.

55

e Who is the Eternal Truth hath, from the Day Spring of Glory, directed His eyes towards the people of Bahá,* and is addressing them in these words: "Address yourselves to the promotion of the well-being and tranquillity of the children of men. Bend your minds and wills to the education of the peoples and kindreds of the earth, that haply the dissensions that divide it may, through the power of the Most Great Name, be blotted out from its face, and all mankind become the upholders of one Order, and the inhabitants of one City. Illumine and hallow your hearts; let them not be profaned by the thorns of hate or the thistles of

---

* Literally, glory, splendor, light; an allusion to Bahá'u'lláh.

malice. Ye dwell in one world, and have been created through the operation of one Will. Blessed is he who mingleth with all men in a spirit of utmost kindliness and love."

56

ime and again have We admonished Our beloved ones to avoid, nay to flee from, anything whatsoever from which the odor of mischief can be detected. The world is in great turmoil, and the minds of its people are in a state of utter confusion. We entreat the Almighty that He may graciously illuminate them with the glory of His Justice, and enable them to discover that which will be profitable unto them at all times and under all conditions. He, verily is the All-Possessing, the Most High.

57

It is incumbent upon every man, in this Day, to hold fast unto whatsoever will promote the interests, and exalt the station, of all nations and just governments. Through each and every one of the verses which the Pen of the Most High hath revealed, the doors of love and unity have been unlocked and flung open to the face of men. We have erewhile declared—and Our Word is the truth—: "Consort with the followers of all religions in a spirit of friendliness and fellowship." Whatsoever hath led the children of men to shun one another, and hath caused dissensions and divisions amongst them, hath, through the revelation of these words, been nullified and abolished.

58

ll men have been created to carry forward an ever-advancing civilization. The Almighty beareth Me witness: To act like the beasts of the field is unworthy of man. Those virtues that befit his dignity are forbearance, mercy, compassion and loving-kindness towards all the peoples and kindreds of the earth. Say: O friends! Drink your fill from this crystal stream that floweth through the heavenly grace of Him Who is the Lord of Names. Let others partake of its waters in My name, that the leaders of men in every land may fully recognize the purpose for which the Eternal Truth hath been revealed, and the reason for which they themselves have been created.

59

hoso cleaveth to justice, can, under no circumstances, transgress the limits of moderation. He discerneth the truth in all things, through the guidance of Him Who is the All-Seeing. The civilization, so often vaunted by the learned exponents of arts and sciences, will, if allowed to overleap the bounds of moderation, bring great evil upon men. Thus warneth you He Who is the All-Knowing. If carried to excess, civilization will prove as prolific a source of evil as it had been of goodness when kept within the restraints of moderation. Meditate on this, O people, and be not of them that wander distraught in the wilderness of error. The day is approaching when its flame will devour the cities, when the Tongue of Grandeur will proclaim: "The Kingdom is God's, the Almighty, the All-Praised!"

All other things are subject to this same principle of moderation. Render thanks unto thy Lord Who hath remembered thee in this wondrous Tablet. All-Praise be to God, the Lord of the glorious throne.

60

ehold the disturbances which, for many a long year, have afflicted the earth, and the perturbation that hath seized its peoples. It hath either been ravaged by war, or tormented by sudden and unforeseen calamities. Though the world is encompassed with misery and distress, yet no man hath paused to reflect what the cause or source of that may be. Whenever the True Counselor uttered a word in admonishment, lo, they all denounced Him as a mover of mischief and rejected His claim. How bewildering, how confusing is such behavior! No two men can be found who may be said to be outwardly and inwardly united. The evidences of discord and malice are apparent everywhere, though all were made for harmony and union. The Great Being saith: O well-beloved ones!

The tabernacle of unity hath been raised; regard ye not one another as strangers. Ye are the fruits of one tree, and the leaves of one branch. We cherish the hope that the light of justice may shine upon the world and sanctify it from tyranny. If the rulers and kings of the earth, the symbols of the power of God, exalted be His glory, arise and resolve to dedicate themselves to whatever will promote the highest interests of the whole of humanity, the reign of justice will assuredly be established amongst the children of men, and the effulgence of its light will envelop the whole earth. The Great Being saith: The structure of world stability and order hath been reared upon, and will continue to be sustained by, the twin pillars of reward and punishment. . . . In another passage He hath written: Take heed, O concourse of the rulers of the world! There is no force on earth that can equal in its conquering power the force of justice and wisdom. . . .

61

 ye the elected representatives of the people in every land! Take ye counsel together, and let your concern be only for that which profiteth mankind and bettereth the condition thereof, if ye be of them that scan heedfully. Regard the world as the human body which, though at its creation whole and perfect, hath been afflicted, through various causes, with grave disorders and maladies. Not for one day did it gain ease, nay its sickness waxed more severe, as it fell under the treatment of ignorant physicians, who gave full rein to their personal desires and have erred grievously. And if, at one time, through the care of an able physician, a member of that body was healed, the rest remained afflicted as before. Thus informeth you the All-Knowing, the All-Wise.

behold it, in this day, at the mercy of rulers so
with pride that they cannot discern clearly their
st advantage, much less recognize a Revelation
ldering and challenging as this. And whenever
of them hath striven to improve its
condition, his motive hath been his own gain,
whether confessedly so or not; and the unworthiness
of this motive hath limited his power to heal or cure.

62

kings of Christendom! . . .

God hath committed into your hands the reins of the government of the people, that ye may rule with justice over them, safeguard the rights of the downtrodden, and punish the wrongdoers. If ye neglect the duty prescribed unto you by God in His Book, your names shall be numbered with those of the unjust in His sight. Grievous, indeed, will be your error. Cleave ye to that which your imaginations have devised, and cast behind your backs the commandments of God, the Most Exalted, the Inaccessible, the All-Compelling, the Almighty? Cast away the things ye possess, and cling to that which God hath bidden you observe. Seek ye His grace, for he that seeketh it treadeth His straight Path.

63

ay not aside the fear of God, O kings of the earth, and beware that ye transgress not the bounds which the Almighty hath fixed. Observe the injunctions laid upon you in His Book, and take good heed not to overstep their limits. Be vigilant, that ye may not do injustice to anyone, be it to the extent of a grain of mustard seed. Tread ye the path of justice, for this, verily, is the straight path.

Compose your differences and reduce your armaments, that the burden of your expenditures may be lightened, and that your minds and hearts may be tranquillized. Heal the dissensions that divide you, and ye will no longer be in need of any armaments except what the protection of your cities and territories demandeth. Fear ye God, and take heed not to outstrip the bounds of moderation and be numbered among the extravagant. We have learned that ye are increasing your outlay every year, and are laying the burden thereof on your subjects. This, verily, is more than they can bear, and is a grievous injustice. Decide ye justly between men, O kings, and be ye the emblems of justice amongst them. This, if ye judge fairly, is the thing that behooveth you, and beseemeth your station.

Beware not to deal unjustly with anyone that appealeth to you and entereth beneath your shadow. Walk ye in the fear of God, and be ye of them that lead a godly life. Rest not on your power, your armies, and treasures. Put your whole trust and confidence in God, Who hath created you, and seek ye His help in all your affairs. Succor cometh from Him alone. He succoreth whom He willeth with the hosts of the heavens and of the earth.

Know ye that the poor are the trust of God in your midst. Watch that ye betray not His trust, that ye deal not unjustly with them and that ye walk not in the ways of the treacherous. Ye will most certainly be called upon to answer for His trust on the day when the Balance of Justice shall be set, the day when unto everyone shall be rendered his due, when the doings of all men, be they rich or poor, shall be weighed.

If ye pay no heed unto the counsels which, in peerless and unequivocal language, We have revealed in this Tablet, Divine chastisement shall assail you from every direction, and the sentence of His justice shall be pronounced against you. On that day ye shall have no power to resist Him, and shall recognize your own impotence. Have mercy on yourselves and on those beneath you, and judge ye between them according to the precepts prescribed by God in His most holy and exalted Tablet, a Tablet wherein He hath assigned to each and every thing its settled measure, in which He hath given, with distinctness, an explanation of all things, and which is in itself a monition unto them that believe in Him.

64

 ow often have things been simple and easy of accomplishment, and yet most men have been heedless, and busied themselves with that which wasteth their time!

65

 ye rulers of the earth! Wherefore have ye clouded the radiance of the Sun, and caused it to cease from shining? Hearken unto the counsel given you by the Pen of the Most High, that haply both ye and the poor may attain unto tranquillity and peace. We beseech God to assist the kings of the earth to establish peace on earth. He, verily, doth what He willeth.

O kings of the earth! We see you increasing every year your expenditures, and laying the burden thereof on your subjects. This, verily, is wholly and grossly unjust. Fear the sighs and tears of this Wronged One, and lay not excessive burdens on your peoples. Do not rob them to rear palaces for yourselves; nay rather choose for them that which ye choose for yourselves. Thus We unfold to your eyes that which profiteth you, if ye but perceive. Your people are your treasures. Beware lest your rule violate the commandments of God, and ye deliver your wards to the hands of the robber. By them ye rule, by their means ye subsist, by their aid ye conquer. Yet, how disdainfully ye look upon them! How strange, how very strange! . . .

Be united, O kings of the earth, for thereby will the tempest of discord be stilled amongst you, and your peoples find rest, if ye be of them that comprehend. Should any one among you take up arms against another, rise ye all against him, for this is naught but manifest justice.

66

hat mankind needeth in this day is
obedience unto them that are in authority,
and a faithful adherence to the cord of
wisdom. The instruments which are
essential to the immediate protection, the security and
assurance of the human race have been entrusted to
the hands, and lie in the grasp, of the governors of
human society. This is the wish of God and His
decree. . . . We cherish the hope that one of the kings
of the earth will, for the sake of God, arise for the
triumph of this wronged, this oppressed people. Such
a king will be eternally extolled and glorified. God
hath prescribed unto this people the duty of aiding
whosoever will aid them, of serving his best interests,
and of demonstrating to him their abiding loyalty.
They who follow Me must strive, under all

circumstances, to promote the welfare of whosoever will arise for the triumph of My Cause, and must at all times prove their devotion and fidelity unto him. Happy is the man that hearkeneth and observeth My counsel. Woe unto him that faileth to fulfill My wish.

67

hed not the blood of anyone, O people, neither judge ye anyone unjustly. Thus have ye been commanded by Him Who knoweth, Who is informed of all. They that commit disorders in the land after it hath been well ordered, these indeed have outstepped the bounds that have been set in the Book. Wretched shall be the abode of the transgressors!

68

OPPRESSORS ON EARTH!

Withdraw your hands from tyranny, for I have pledged Myself not to forgive any man's injustice. This is My covenant which I have irrevocably decreed in the preserved tablet and sealed with My seal.

69

 e entreat God to deliver the light of equity and the sun of justice from the thick clouds of waywardness, and cause them to shine forth upon men. No light can compare with the light of justice. The establishment of order in the world and the tranquillity of the nations depend upon it.

70

e fair to yourselves and to others, that the evidences of justice may be revealed, through your deeds, among Our faithful servants. Beware lest ye encroach upon the substance of your neighbor. Prove yourselves worthy of his trust and confidence in you, and withhold not from the poor the gifts which the grace of God hath bestowed upon you. He, verily, shall recompense the charitable, and doubly repay them for what they have bestowed. No God is there but Him. All creation and its empire are His. He bestoweth His gifts on whom He will, and from whom He will He withholdeth them. He is the Great Giver, the Most Generous, the Benevolent.

71

he Daystar of Truth that shineth in its meridian splendor beareth Us witness! They who are the people of God have no ambition except to revive the world, to ennoble its life, and regenerate its peoples. Truthfulness and goodwill have, at all times, marked their relations with all men. Their outward conduct is but a reflection of their inward life, and their inward life a mirror of their outward conduct. No veil hideth or obscureth the verities on which their Faith is established. Before the eyes of all men these verities have been laid bare, and can be unmistakably recognized. Their very acts attest the truth of these words.

72

ith the utmost friendliness and in a spirit of perfect fellowship take ye counsel together and dedicate the precious days of your lives to the betterment of the world and the promotion of the Cause of Him Who is the Ancient and Sovereign Lord of all. He, verily, enjoineth upon all men what is right, and forbiddeth whatsoever degradeth their station.

73

"This is the day to make mention of God, to celebrate His praise, and to serve Him; deprive not yourselves thereof. Ye are the letters of the words, and the words of the Book. Ye are the saplings which the hand of Loving-kindness hath planted in the soil of mercy, and which the showers of bounty have made to flourish. He hath protected you from the mighty winds of misbelief, and the tempestuous gales of impiety, and nurtured you with the hands of His loving providence. Now is the time for you to put forth your leaves, and yield your fruit. The fruits of the tree of man have ever been and are goodly deeds and a praiseworthy character."

The Soul of Man

74

hoso hath, in this Day, refused to allow the doubts and fancies of men to turn him away from Him Who is the Eternal Truth, and hath not suffered the tumult provoked by the ecclesiastical and secular authorities to deter him from recognizing His Message, such a man will be regarded by God, the Lord of all men, as one of His mighty signs, and will be numbered among them whose names have been inscribed by the Pen of the Most High in His Book. Blessed is he that hath recognized the true stature of such a soul, that hath acknowledged its station, and discovered its virtues.

75

 very soul that walketh humbly with its God, in this Day, and cleaveth unto Him, shall find itself invested with the honor and glory of all goodly names and stations.

76

ert thou to attain to but a dewdrop of the crystal waters of divine knowledge, thou wouldst readily realize that true life is not the life of the flesh but the life of the spirit. For the life of the flesh is common to both men and animals, whereas the life of the spirit is possessed only by the pure in heart who have quaffed from the ocean of faith and partaken of the fruit of certitude. This life knoweth no death, and this existence is crowned by immortality. Even as it hath been said: "He who is a true believer liveth both in this world and in the world to come."

77

ust as the conception of faith hath existed from the beginning that hath no beginning, and will endure till the end that hath no end, in like manner will the true believer eternally live and endure. His spirit will everlastingly circle round the Will of God. He will last as long as God, Himself, will last. He is revealed through the Revelation of God, and is hidden at His bidding. It is evident that the loftiest mansions in the Realm of Immortality have been ordained as the habitation of them that have truly believed in God and in His signs. Death can never invade that holy seat. Thus have We entrusted thee with the signs of thy Lord, that thou mayest persevere in thy love for Him, and be of them that comprehend this truth.

78

t is clear and evident that all men shall, after their physical death, estimate the worth of their deeds, and realize all that their hands have wrought. I swear by the Daystar that shineth above the horizon of Divine power! They that are the followers of the one true God shall, the moment they depart out of this life, experience such joy and gladness as would be impossible to describe, while they that live in error shall be seized with such fear and trembling, and shall be filled with such consternation, as nothing can exceed. Well is it with him that hath quaffed the choice and incorruptible wine of faith through the gracious favor and the manifold bounties of Him Who is the Lord of all Faiths. . . .

79

now thou that every hearing ear, if kept pure and undulled, must, at all times and from every direction, hearken to the voice that uttereth these holy words: "Verily, we are God's, and to Him shall we return." The mysteries of man's physical death and of his return have not been divulged, and still remain unread. By the righteousness of God! Were they to be revealed, they would woke such fear and sorrow that some would perish, while others would be so filled with gladness as to wish for death, and beseech, with unceasing longing, the one true God—exalted be His glory—to hasten their end.

Death proffereth unto every confident believer the cup that is life indeed. It bestoweth joy, and is the bearer of gladness. It conferreth the gift of everlasting life.

As to those that have tasted of the fruit of man's earthly existence, which is the recognition of the one true God, exalted be His glory, their life hereafter is such as We are unable to describe. The knowledge thereof is with God, alone, the Lord of all worlds.

80

he nature of the soul after death can never be described, nor is it meet and permissible to reveal its whole character to the eyes of men. The Prophets and Messengers of God have been sent down for the sole purpose of guiding mankind to the straight Path of Truth. The purpose underlying Their revelation hath been to educate all men, that they may, at the hour of death, ascend, in the utmost purity and sanctity and with absolute detachment, to the throne of the Most High.

81

hou hast, moreover, asked Me concerning the state of the soul after its separation from the body. Know thou, of a truth, that if the soul of man hath walked in the ways of God, it will, assuredly, return and be gathered to the glory of the Beloved. By the righteousness of God! It shall attain a station such as no pen can depict, or tongue describe. The soul that hath remained faithful to the Cause of God, and stood unwaveringly firm in His Path shall, after his ascension, be possessed of such power that all the worlds which the Almighty hath created can benefit through him. Such a soul provideth, at the bidding of the Ideal King and Divine Educator, the pure leaven that leaveneth the world of being, and furnisheth the power through which the arts and wonders of the world are made manifest. Consider how meal needeth leaven to be leavened with. Those souls that are the symbols of detachment are the leaven of the world. Meditate on this, and be of the thankful.

82

 SON OF MAN!

Thou art My dominion and My dominion perisheth not; wherefore fearest thou thy perishing? Thou art My light and My light shall never be extinguished; why dost thou dread extinction? Thou art My glory and My glory fadeth not; thou art My robe and My robe shall never be outworn. Abide then in thy love for Me, that thou mayest find Me in the realm of glory.

The Covenant Renewed

83

SON OF MAN!

Veiled in My immemorial being and in the ancient eternity of My essence, I knew My love for thee; therefore I created thee, have engraved on thee Mine image and revealed to thee My beauty.

84

SON OF BEING!

Love Me, that I may love thee. If thou lovest
Me not, My love can in no wise reach thee.
Know this, O servant

85

 testify, O my God, that this is the Day
whereon Thy testimony hath been fulfilled,
and Thy clear tokens have been manifested,
and Thine utterances have been revealed,
and Thy signs have been demonstrated, and the
radiance of Thy countenance hath been diffused, and
Thy proof hath been perfected, and Thine ascendancy
hath been established, and Thy mercy hath
overflowed, and the Daystar of Thy grace hath shone
forth with such brilliance that Thou didst manifest
Him Who is the Revealer of Thyself and the Treasury
of Thy wisdom and the Dawning-Place of Thy
majesty and power. Thou didst establish His covenant
with every one who hath been created in the
kingdoms of earth and heaven and in the realms of
revelation and of creation. Thou didst raise Him up

to such heights that the wrongs inflicted by the oppressors have been powerless to deter Him from revealing Thy sovereignty, and the ascendancy of the wayward hath failed to prevent Him from demonstrating Thy power and from exalting Thy Cause.

86

lorified art Thou, O my God! Thou knowest that my sole aim in revealing Thy Cause hath been to reveal Thee and not my self, and to manifest Thy glory rather than my glory.

87

nd when the entire creation was stirred up, and the whole earth was convulsed, and the sweet savors of Thy name, the All-Praised, had almost ceased to breathe over Thy realms, and the winds of Thy mercy had well-nigh been stilled throughout Thy dominions, Thou didst, through the power of Thy might, raise me up among Thy servants, and bid me to show forth Thy sovereignty amidst Thy people. Thereupon I arose before all Thy creatures, strengthened by Thy help and Thy power, and summoned all the multitudes unto Thee, and announced unto all Thy servants Thy favors and Thy gifts, and invited them to turn towards this Ocean, every drop of the waters of which crieth out, proclaiming unto all that are in heaven and on earth that He is, in truth, the Fountain of all life, and the Quickener of the entire creation, and the Object of the adoration of all worlds, and the Best-Beloved of every understanding heart, and the Desire of all them that are nigh unto Thee.

88

I beseech Thee, by Thy Most Great Name, to open the eyes of Thy servants, that they may behold Thee shining above the horizon of Thy majesty and glory, and that they may not be hindered by the croaking of the raven from hearkening to the voice of the Dove of Thy sublime oneness, nor be prevented by the corrupt waters from partaking of the pure wine of Thy bounty and the everlasting streams of Thy gifts.

Gather them, then, together around this Divine Law, the covenant of which Thou hast established with all Thy Prophets and Thy Messengers, and Whose ordinances Thou hast written down in Thy Tablets and Thy Scriptures. Raise them up, moreover, to such heights as will enable them to perceive Thy Call.

Potent art Thou to do what pleaseth Thee. Thou art, verily, the Inaccessible, the All-Glorious.

89

ay: O people! The Day, promised unto you in all the Scriptures, is now come. Fear ye God, and withhold not yourselves from recognizing the One Who is the Object of your creation. Hasten ye unto Him. Better is this for you than the world and all that is therein. Would that ye could perceive it!

90

hat which is conducive to the regeneration of the world and the salvation of the peoples and kindreds of the earth hath been sent down from the heaven of the utterance of Him Who is the Desire of the world. Give ye a hearing ear to the counsels of the Pen of Glory. Better is this for you than all that is on the earth. Unto this beareth witness My glorious and wondrous Book.

91

he Day whereon ye can behold the Promised One and attain unto Him hath drawn nigh! O followers of the Gospel! Prepare the way! The Day of the advent of the Glorious Lord is at hand! Make ready to enter the Kingdom. Thus hath it been ordained by God, He Who causeth the dawn to break.

Give ear unto that which the Dove of Eternity warbleth upon the twigs of the Divine Lote-Tree: O peoples of the earth! We sent forth him who was named John to baptize you with water, that your bodies might be cleansed for the appearance of the Messiah. He, in turn, purified you with the fire of love and the water of the spirit in anticipation of these Days whereon the All-Merciful hath purposed to cleanse you with the water of life at the hands of His loving providence. This is the Father foretold by Isaiah, and the Comforter concerning Whom the Spirit had covenanted with you. . . .

Say: O peoples of all faiths! . . . The Ancient Beauty is come in His Most Great Name, and He wisheth to admit all mankind into His most holy Kingdom. The pure in heart behold the Kingdom of God manifest before His Face. . . . He, verily, hath come again that ye might be redeemed, O peoples of the earth.

O people! Hearken unto that which hath been revealed by your All-Glorious Lord, and turn your faces unto God, the Lord of this world and of the world to come. Thus doth He Who is the Dawning-Place of the Daystar of divine inspiration command you as bidden by the Fashioner of all mankind. We, verily, have created you for the light, and desire not to abandon you unto the fire. Come forth, O people, from darkness by the grace of this Sun which hath shone forth above the horizon of divine providence, and turn thereunto with sanctified hearts and assured souls, with seeing eyes and beaming faces. Thus counseleth you the Supreme Ordainer from the scene of His transcendent glory, that perchance His summons may draw you nigh unto the Kingdom of His names.

References

1. Bahá'u'lláh, quoted in Shoghi Effendi, *The Advent of Divine Justice*, p. 77.
2. Bahá'u'lláh, quoted in Shoghi Effendi, *The Advent of Divine Justice*, p. 78.
3. Bahá'u'lláh, quoted in Shoghi Effendi, *The Advent of Divine Justice*, p. 79.
4. Bahá'u'lláh, quoted in Shoghi Effendi, *The Advent of Divine Justice*, p. 79.
5. Bahá'u'lláh, quoted in Shoghi Effendi, *The Advent of Divine Justice*, pp. 79–80.
6. Bahá'u'lláh, *Gleanings from the Writings of Bahá'u'lláh*, p. 340.
7. Bahá'u'lláh, *Prayers and Meditations*, p. 152.
8. Bahá'u'lláh, *Prayers and Meditations*, p. 94.
9. Bahá'u'lláh, *Prayers and Meditations*, pp. 86–87.
10. Bahá'u'lláh, *Gleanings from the Writings of Bahá'u'lláh*, pp. 3–4.
11. Bahá'u'lláh, *Prayers and Meditations*, p. 128.
12. Bahá'u'lláh, *Gleanings from the Writings of Bahá'u'lláh*, p. 49.
13. Bahá'u'lláh, *The Kitáb-i-Íqán*, ¶106.
14. Bahá'u'lláh, *Gleanings from the Writings of Bahá'u'lláh*, pp. 78–79.
15. Bahá'u'lláh, *Gleanings from the Writings of Bahá'u'lláh*, pp. 59–60.

16. Bahá'u'lláh, *Gleanings from the Writings of Bahá'u'lláh*, pp. 67–68.

17. Bahá'u'lláh, *Gleanings from the Writings of Bahá'u'lláh*, p. 5.

18. Bahá'u'lláh, *The Kitáb-i-Íqán*, ¶1–2.

19. Bahá'u'lláh, *The Kitáb-i-Íqán*, ¶76.

20. Bahá'u'lláh, *Gleanings from the Writings of Bahá'u'lláh*, pp. 175–77.

21. Bahá'u'lláh, *Epistle to the Son of the Wolf*, p. 83.

22. Bahá'u'lláh, *Gleanings from the Writings of Bahá'u'lláh*, p. 261.

23. Bahá'u'lláh, *Gleanings from the Writings of Bahá'u'lláh*, pp. 271–72.

24. Bahá'u'lláh, *Gleanings from the Writings of Bahá'u'lláh*, p. 272.

25. Bahá'u'lláh, *Gleanings from the Writings of Bahá'u'lláh*, p. 36.

26. Bahá'u'lláh, *Gleanings from the Writings of Bahá'u'lláh*, pp. 279–80.

27. Bahá'u'lláh, *Gleanings from the Writings of Bahá'u'lláh*, p. 186.

28. Bahá'u'lláh, *Gleanings from the Writings of Bahá'u'lláh*, pp. 34–35

29. Bahá'u'lláh, *Gleanings from the Writings of Bahá'u'lláh*, p. 143.

30. Bahá'u'lláh, *Gleanings from the Writings of Bahá'u'lláh*, p. 149.

31. Bahá'u'lláh, *Gleanings from the Writings of Bahá'u'lláh*, pp. 167–68.

32. Bahá'u'lláh, *The Kitáb-i-Aqdas*, ¶161–63.

33. Bahá'u'lláh, *Gleanings from the Writings of Bahá'u'lláh*, pp. 289–90.

34. Bahá'u'lláh, *The Kitáb-i-Aqdas*, ¶7.

35. Bahá'u'lláh, *Gleanings from the Writings of Bahá'u'lláh*, p. 276.

36. Bahá'u'lláh, *The Kitáb-i-Íqán*, ¶213–14.

37. Bahá'u'lláh, *Epistle to the Son of the Wolf*, p. 93.

38. Bahá'u'lláh, *Gleanings from the Writings of Bahá'u'lláh*, p. 297.

39. Bahá'u'lláh, *The Seven Valleys and the Four Valleys*, p. 6.

40. Bahá'u'lláh, *Gleanings from the Writings of Bahá'u'lláh*, p. 305.

41. Bahá'u'lláh, *Epistle to the Son of the Wolf*, p. 29.

42. Bahá'u'lláh, *Gleanings from the Writings of Bahá'u'lláh*, p. 338.

43. Bahá'u'lláh, *Gleanings from the Writings of Bahá'u'lláh*, p. 329.

44. Bahá'u'lláh, *Gleanings from the Writings of Bahá'u'lláh*, p. 319.

45. Bahá'u'lláh, *Epistle to the Son of the Wolf*, p. 24.

46. Bahá'u'lláh, *Gleanings from the Writings of Bahá'u'lláh*, p. 213.

47. Bahá'u'lláh, *Epistle to the Son of the Wolf*, pp. 62–63.

48. Bahá'u'lláh, *Gleanings from the Writings of Bahá'u'lláh*, pp. 80–81.

49. Bahá'u'lláh, *Gleanings from the Writings of Bahá'u'lláh*, pp. 99–100.

50. Bahá'u'lláh, *Gleanings from the Writings of Bahá'u'lláh*, pp. 286–87.

51. Bahá'u'lláh, *Tablets of Bahá'u'lláh*, pp. 84–86.

52. Bahá'u'lláh, *Epistle to the Son of the Wolf*, pp. 13–14.

53. Bahá'u'lláh, *The Kitáb-i-Aqdas*, ¶58.

54. Bahá'u'lláh, *Gleanings from the Writings of Bahá'u'lláh*, p. 196.

55. Bahá'u'lláh, *Gleanings from the Writings of Bahá'u'lláh*, pp. 333–34.

56. Bahá'u'lláh, *Tablets of Bahá'u'lláh*, p. 94.

57. Bahá'u'lláh, *Tablets of Bahá'u'lláh*, p. 87.

58. Bahá'u'lláh, *Gleanings from the Writings of Bahá'u'lláh*, p. 215.

59. Bahá'u'lláh, *Gleanings from the Writings of Bahá'u'lláh*, pp. 342–43.

60. Bahá'u'lláh, *Tablets of Bahá'u'lláh*, pp. 163–64.

61. Bahá'u'lláh, *The Summons of the Lord of Hosts*, Súriy-i-Haykal, ¶174–75.

62. Bahá'u'lláh, *The Summons of the Lord of Hosts*, Súriy-i-Mulúk, ¶15, ¶21.

63. Bahá'u'lláh, *The Summons of the Lord of Hosts*, Súriy-i-Mulúk, ¶7–8, ¶10–12.

64. Bahá'u'lláh, *Epistle to the Son of the Wolf*, p. 137.

65. Bahá'u'lláh, *The Summons of the Lord of Hosts*, Súriy-i-Haykal, ¶178–182.

66. Bahá'u'lláh, *Gleanings from the Writings of Bahá'u'lláh*, p. 207.

67. Bahá'u'lláh, *The Summons of the Lord of Hosts*, Súriy-i-Haykal, ¶147.

68. Bahá'u'lláh, *The Hidden Words*, Persian, no. 64.

69. Bahá'u'lláh, *Epistle to the Son of the Wolf*, pp. 28–29.

70. Bahá'u'lláh, *Gleanings from the Writings of Bahá'u'lláh*, p. 278.

71. Bahá'u'lláh, *Gleanings from the Writings of Bahá'u'lláh*, pp. 270–71.

72. Bahá'u'lláh, *Gleanings from the Writings of Bahá'u'lláh*, p. 184.

73. Bahá'u'lláh, *Epistle to the Son of the Wolf*, p. 25–26.

74. Bahá'u'lláh, *Gleanings from the Writings of Bahá'u'lláh*, p. 159.

75. Bahá'u'lláh, *Gleanings from the Writings of Bahá'u'lláh*, p. 159.

76. Bahá'u'lláh, *The Kitáb-i-Íqán*, ¶128.

77. Bahá'u'lláh, *Gleanings from the Writings of Bahá'u'lláh*, p. 141.

78. Bahá'u'lláh, *Gleanings from the Writings of Bahá'u'lláh*, p. 171.

79. Bahá'u'lláh, *Gleanings from the Writings of Bahá'u'lláh*, pp. 345–346.

80. Bahá'u'lláh, *Gleanings from the Writings of Bahá'u'lláh*, pp. 156–57.

81. Bahá'u'lláh, *Gleanings from the Writings of Bahá'u'lláh*, p. 161.

82. Bahá'u'lláh, *The Hidden Words*, Arabic, no. 14.

83. Bahá'u'lláh, *The Hidden Words*, Arabic, no. 3.

84. Bahá'u'lláh, *The Hidden Words*, Arabic, no. 5.

85. Bahá'u'lláh, *Prayers and Meditations*, pp. 35–36.

86. Bahá'u'lláh, *Prayers and Meditations*, p. 103.

87. Bahá'u'lláh, *Prayers and Meditations*, p. 104.

88. Bahá'u'lláh, *Prayers and Meditations*, p. 106.

89. Bahá'u'lláh, *Gleanings from the Writings of Bahá'u'lláh*, p. 314.

90. Bahá'u'lláh, *Tablets of Bahá'u'lláh*, p. 223.

91. Bahá'u'lláh, *The Summons of the Lord of Hosts*, ¶121–24.

Bibliography

Works of Bahá'u'lláh

Epistle to the Son of the Wolf. 1st pocket-size ed. Translated by Shoghi Effendi. Wilmette, IL: Bahá'í Publishing Trust, 1988.

Gleanings from the Writings of Bahá'u'lláh. 1st pocket-size ed. Translated by Shoghi Effendi. Wilmette, IL: Bahá'í Publishing Trust, 1983.

The Hidden Words. Translated by Shoghi Effendi. Wilmette, IL: Bahá'í Publishing, 2002.

The Kitáb-i-Aqdas: The Most Holy Book. 1st pocket-size ed. Wilmette, IL: Bahá'í Publishing Trust, 1993.

The Kitáb-i-Íqán: The Book of Certitude. Translated by Shoghi Effendi. Wilmette, IL: Bahá'í Publishing, 2003.

Prayers and Meditations. Translated by Shoghi Effendi. 1st pocket-size ed. Wilmette, IL: Bahá'í Publishing Trust, 1987.

The Seven Valleys and the Four Valleys. New ed. Translated by Ali-Kuli Khan and Marzieh Gail. Wilmette, IL: Bahá'í Publishing Trust, 1991.

The Summons of the Lord of Hosts: Tablets of Bahá'u'lláh. Haifa: Bahá'í World Centre, 2002.

Works of Shoghi Effendi

The Advent of Divine Justice. 1st pocket-size ed. Wilmette, IL:
Bahá'í Publishing Trust, 1990.

The World Order of Bahá'u'lláh: Selected Letters. 1st pocket-size ed.
Wilmette, IL: Bahá'í Publishing Trust, 1991.

A Basic Bahá'í Reading List

The following list provides a sampling of works conveying the spiritual truths, social principles, and history of the Bahá'í Faith.

Introductory Works

Bahá'í International Community, Office of Public Information, New York. *Bahá'u'lláh*. Wilmette, IL: Bahá'í Publishing Trust, 1991.

Bowers, Kenneth E. *God Speaks Again: An Introduction to the Bahá'í Faith*. Wilmette, IL: Bahá'í Publishing, 2004.

Hatcher, William S., and J. Douglas Martin. *The Bahá'í Faith: The Emerging Global Religion*. Wilmette, IL: Bahá'í Publishing, 2002.

Smith, Peter. *A Concise Encyclopedia of the Bahá'í Faith*. Oxford: Oneworld Publications, 2000.

Selected Writings of Bahá'u'lláh

Gleanings from the Writings of Bahá'u'lláh. 1st ps ed. Translated by Shoghi Effendi. Wilmette, IL: Bahá'í Publishing Trust, 1983.

The Hidden Words. Translated by Shoghi Effendi. Wilmette, IL: Bahá'í Publishing, 2002.

The Kitáb-i-Aqdas: The Most Holy Book. Wilmette, IL: Bahá'í Publishing Trust, 1993.

The Kitáb-i-Íqán: The Book of Certitude. 1st ps ed. Translated by Shoghi Effendi. Wilmette, IL: Bahá'í Publishing, 2003.

Tablets of Bahá'u'lláh revealed after the Kitáb-i-Aqdas. Compiled by the Research Department of the Universal House of Justice. Translated by Habib Taherzadeh. 1st ps ed. Wilmette, IL: Bahá'í Publishing Trust, 1998.

Selected Writings of 'Abdu'l-Bahá

Paris Talks: Addresses given by 'Abdu'l-Bahá in Paris in 1911. 12th ed. London: Bahá'í Publishing Trust, 1995.

The Promulgation of Universal Peace: Talks Delivered by 'Abdu'l-Bahá during His Visit to the United States and Canada in 1912. Compiled by Howard MacNutt. 2nd ed. Wilmette, IL: Bahá'í Publishing Trust, 1982.

The Secret of Divine Civilization. 1st ps ed. Translated by Marzieh Gail and Ali-Kuli Khán. Wilmette, IL: Bahá'í Publishing Trust, 1990.

Selections from the Writings of 'Abdu'l-Bahá. Compiled by the Research Department of the Universal House of Justice. Translated by a Committee at the Bahá'í World Center and Marzieh Gail. Wilmette, IL: Bahá'í Publishing Trust, 1997.

Some Answered Questions. Compiled and translated by Laura Clifford Barney. 1st ps ed. Wilmette, IL: Bahá'í Publishing Trust, 1984.

Index

For more information about the Bahá'í Faith,
or to contact the Bahá'ís near you,
visit http://www.us.bahai.org/
or call
1-800-22-UNITE

Bahá'í Publishing
and the Bahá'í Faith

Bahá'í Publishing produces books based on the teachings of the Bahá'í Faith. Founded nearly 160 years ago, the Bahá'í Faith has spread to some 235 nations and territories and is now accepted by more than five million people. The word "Bahá'í" means "follower of Bahá'u'lláh." Bahá'u'lláh, the founder of the Bahá'í Faith, asserted that he is the Messenger of God for all of humanity in this day. The cornerstone of his teachings is the establishment of the spiritual unity of humankind, which will be achieved by personal transformation and the application of clearly identified spiritual principles. Bahá'ís also believe that there is but one religion and that all the Messengers of God— among them Abraham, Zoroaster, Moses, Krishna, Buddha, Jesus, and Muḥammad—have progressively revealed its nature. Together, the world's great religions are expressions of a single, unfolding divine plan. Human beings, not God's Messengers, are the source of religious divisions, prejudices, and hatreds.

The Bahá'í Faith is not a sect or denomination of another religion, nor is it a cult or a social movement. Rather, it is a globally recognized independent world religion founded on new books of scripture revealed by Bahá'u'lláh.

Bahá'í Publishing is an imprint of the National Spiritual Assembly of the Bahá'ís of the United States.

Other Books Available from Bahá'í Publishing

The Challenge of Bahá'u'lláh

by Gary L. Matthews

Members of the Bahá'í Faith, the youngest of the independent world religions, represent one of the most culturally, geographically, and economically diverse groups of people on the planet, yet all are firmly united in their belief that the prophet and founder of their faith—Bahá'u'lláh (1817–1892), a Persian nobleman by birth—is none other than the "Promised One" prophesied in the scriptures of the world's great religions. Bahá'u'lláh Himself claimed to be the Messenger of God for humanity in this day, the bearer of a new revelation from God that will transform the human race.

Author Gary Matthews addresses the central question that anyone investigating the life, character, and writings of Bahá'u'lláh must ask: Is this remarkable figure really Who He claims to be? The author explains why he believes the revelation of Bahá'u'lláh is not only divine in origin, but also represents a unique challenge of unequaled importance to humanity today.

Matthews sets forth the claims of Bahá'u'lláh, summarizes His teachings, and then embarks on his own examination. His investigation correlates Bahá'í prophecies with developments in history and science; considers Bahá'u'lláh's knowledge, wisdom, and character; describes His ability to reveal scripture and what it was like to be in His presence; discusses the profound influence of His writings; and more. Matthews concludes by inviting readers to make their own analysis of the record.

$15.00 / $18.00 CAN
ISBN 1-931847-16-9

Close Connections: The Bridge between Spiritual and Physical Reality

by John S. Hatcher

Is consciousness a product of the soul or an illusion the brain creates? Has creation always existed, or does it have a point of beginning? Is matter infinitely refinable, or is there some indivisible building block for all of physical creation? Is the universe infinite or a finite "closed" system? Has the human being always been a distinct creation, or did we evolve from a lesser species? Is there a Creator whose design has guided the evolution of human society, or did creation and human society come about by pure chance? And if there is a Creator, why does He seem to allow injustice to thrive and the innocent to suffer so that we call natural disasters "acts of God"?

In *Close Connections* author and scholar John Hatcher employs axioms drawn from the Bahá'í Faith as tools for probing answers to these and other questions that relate to one overriding question: What is the purpose of physical reality? At the heart of the quest for these answers is a provocative analogy—a comparison of the creation and functioning of the individual human being with the method by which creation as a whole has come into being and progresses towards some as yet concealed destiny.

If the conclusions Hatcher draws from this study are correct, then every branch of science must in time reconsider its understanding of reality to include at least one additional dimension—the metaphysical or spiritual dimension—and its relationship to, and influence on, material reality.

$20.00 / $24.00 CAN
ISBN 1-931847-15-0

Prophet's Daughter: The Life and Legacy of Bahíyyih Khánum, Outstanding Heroine of the Bahá'í Faith

by Janet A. Khan

The remarkable story of a woman who shaped the course of religious history.

Prophet's Daughter examines the extraordinary life of Bahíyyih Khánum (1846–1932), the daughter of Bahá'u'lláh, founder of the Bahá'í Faith. During the mid-nineteenth and early twentieth centuries, when women in the Middle East were largely invisible, deprived of education, and without status in their communities, Bahíyyih Khánum was an active participant in the religion's turbulent early years and contributed significantly both to the development of its administrative structure and to its emergence as a worldwide faith community. Her appointment to head the Bahá'í Faith during a critical period of transition stands unique in religious history.

Bahíyyih Khánum's response to the events in her life despite some eight decades of extreme hardship illustrates her ability to transcend the social and cultural constraints of the traditional Muslim society in which she lived. Optimistic and resilient in the face of relentless persecution and uncertainty, practical and

resourceful by nature, she embraced change, took action, and looked to the future. The legacy of her life offers an inspiring model for thoughtful women and men who seek creative ways to deal with social change and the pressures of contemporary life.
$18.00 / $22.00 CAN
ISBN 1-931847-14-2

The Reality of Man
Compiled by Terry J. Cassiday, Christopher J. Martin, and Bahhaj Taherzadeh

What if it were possible for God to tell us why He created human beings? What if it were possible for Him to tell us the purpose of our existence?

Members of the Bahá'í Faith believe that just such information—and vastly more—is found in the revelation of Bahá'u'lláh, a body of work they consider to be the revealed Word of God. Bahá'u'lláh, Whose given name was Mírzá Ḥusayn-'Alí (1817–1892), was a Persian nobleman Who claimed to receive a new revelation from God fulfilling prophetic expectations of all the major religions while laying the foundation for a world civilization.

The Reality of Man presents a glimpse of the unique depth, range, and creative potency of Bahá'u'lláh's writings on such fundamental questions as What is a human being? What is the purpose of human existence? Where did we come from? Is there a God? What is God like? Do we each have a preordained role or mission in life? Is there life after death? Are some religions "true" and others "false"? How can one evaluate religions? Prepared by the editors at Bahá'í Publishing, this compilation also includes writings from Bahá'u'lláh's eldest son and designated successor, 'Abdu'l-Bahá (1844–1921), whose written works Bahá'ís regard as authoritative.
ISBN 1-931847-17-7
$12.00 / $15.00 CAN

The Story of Bahá'u'lláh:
Promised One of All Religions

by Druzelle Cederquist

From the affluent courtyards of Tehran to the prison-city of Acre on the shores of the Mediterranean, *The Story of Bahá'u'lláh* brings to life in rich detail the compelling story of the prophet and founder of the Bahá'í Faith. Born to wealth and privilege, Bahá'u'lláh (1817–1892) was known as the "Father of the Poor" for His help to the needy. Yet despite His social standing, nothing could stop the forces that would have Him unjustly imprisoned in Tehran's notorious "Black Pit." Upon His release He was banished from Iran on a mountainous winter journey that His enemies hoped would kill Him.

Despite the schemes of His foes and the hardships of His exile, Bahá'u'lláh openly proclaimed the divine guidance revealed to Him. In over one hundred volumes, He delivered teachings on subjects ranging from the nobility of the soul to the prerequisites for the nations of the world to achieve a just and lasting peace.

The heart of His teaching was a new vision of the oneness of humanity and of the divine Messengers—among them Abraham, Moses, Buddha, Krishna, Christ, Muḥammad—Whom He claimed represent one "changeless Faith of God." Their teachings, He asserted, were the energizing force for the advancement of civilization. In 1863 Bahá'u'lláh announced He was the Messenger of God for humanity today and declared that His mission was to usher in the age of peace and prosperity prophesied in the scriptures of the world's great religions.
$15.00 / $18.00 CAN
ISBN 1-931847-13-4